THAT EX

That Ex
© 2020 Rachelle Toarmino

Published by Big Lucks Books
Austin, TX
http://BigLucks.com

Cover and Book Design by Mark Cugini
http://cugini.party

Titles set in Visby; text set in Crimson

Library of Congress Cataloging-in-Publication Data

Toarmino, Rachelle.
That Ex / by Rachelle Toarmino
ISBN-13: 978-1-941985-10-6
ISBN-10: 9781941985106
Library of Congress Control Number: 2020933427

First Edition, June 2020

that ex

RACHELLE TOARMINO

Big Lucks Books, 2020

CONTENTS

for the group chat

"Oh, so it's my fault?"
    —Carmela Soprano

WEEK OF WAKING THOUGHTS

they're leaves because they leave trees

every time you hit snooze there is a child in the world who has
   to get up

no

bitch not this again

inside I am colors flying

mindlessly written in pink and pale gray

there isn't any space here for him or him either

YOU ANIMAL

in the beginning
God felt a little cute
so in His image
He created man
tho He saw that He
might delete later
what good is it to
write about loving
a man when you
have to shake out
the past's pockets
all this making
a show of memory
what kind of
person does that
whenever a girl
changes a contact
in her phone to
DON'T ANSWER
that's the kind of
love I'd write about
not the trying-to-
decode-the-emoji-
on-your-ex's-
recent-Venmo-
transaction kind
you like that
don't you I knew
a man once who

had a tattoo
of Jesus crying
bloody tears on his
arm when we had
sex Jesus shook
his head no well
there are many
ways to love
like Britney that
class act she went
high & shaved her
head for our sins girl
get it but Justin
he was still too
much & for no
good reason!
where I come from
you get knocked
out cold for that
I guess I know
a little thing or two
about a man's
ego how it under-
estimates soul
not every gesture is
a metaphor for how
much the world
respects you it
wasn't supposed

to be like this
now all our loose
ends kneel down
like an unbalanced
equation inside
of me not that I
blame him I too
know the agony
of not being able to
get inside of some-
thing that you feel
drawn by God
to call your home
I could've lived a
whole lifetime in
the way he used to
cherish me how ex-
pensive the hunger
was in his eyes how
it made me feel so
much
try telling him that
anytime you start
dating a new man
you should have to
thank all his exes
for the moisturizer
he uses how he
dresses himself how

he goes down & o!
my loneliness
was killing me
aaaand I
I think there's love
I don't think it's what
we thought it was
I still believe

HARD FEELINGS

feeling old when you open a folder of drafts

your hands and where to put them

your legs and how to lean

writing cover letters
and feeling like you're a product review

thinking your voice sounds unsalted
when you hear it on a recording

feeling lonely inside a furniture store

grief

love

nostalgia

using people as templates
and making them live as characters
or contradictions

getting sad to cope with being bored

wishing you could kill a memory
like hunger

by feeding it

LOVELESS

Somewhere a man owns
exclusive rights to the world's
pinkest pink. Whatever
faith you have is on its way
but hitting every light. All the
right words in the last place
you saw them.

You know who is going
home on *Project Runway*
once the producers show
them mercy. Hours
like an asteroid in
orbit, each lap taking
the edge off.

Which of the following
answers isn't a solution?
Exhausted and *sold out*
are the same word in at
least one language. *Wait*
and *hope. Drowning*
and *going home.*

You're all routine. So
much to lose and nothing
to show for it. So
obsessed are you with
your own fury
that you keep calling it
and hanging up.

CALL IT WHAT YOU WANT

How many times today will you make a cult of grief?

Hack: Call it nostalgia when you let hours happen somewhere else.

Do you think the dark takes it personally? All that animal fear.

Hot as...forget it.

That dream again where you mail postcards to yourself.

Moments so shallow your feet almost touch the bottom.

Go on: Collect at the edge of your shadow. All that plot smacked
out of you.

Staying put. Call it what you want...you are staying where you
were put.

What's the last thing you let do all the talking? This business of
naming things

is the beginning of everything. To feel as neutral as...an expired
coupon!

Thoughts that come from burning are still thoughts.

You hate and love. Longing wants what it wants.

You want for peace to be a matter of quiet.

You want for quiet to be a matter of rolling up all the sidewalks outside.

MEMORIES MOVING BACKWARD

In all of my memories of you, you are moving backward.
Your face pulls open into an armed expression,
and then knows me, and then closes for the first time.

Night is nothing but night in this part of the poem.
You leave one time, a hundred times. Over, all over again.
It's nothing to know how long a night can be.

I could see our love was ending. In my memories of you.
Even grief is desire, even fear. Still it was strange
to watch your face turn to thunder in mine.

A loop of backward traffic: that time we gave up the day,
that time we described the whole night, that time we followed
where the light goes, worshipped some unofficial thing.

I WANTED TO ASK YOU

I wanted to ask you
if you knew how vertically time shifts
when you say *What aren't we doing*

and seem to mean it. I kick
up each word to see
what's underneath and spread

some moments out
onto my lap. There are mornings
spent in quiet violence

and movements made
inside light. Bluish shadows
stripe the last shreds of sunlight

through blinds onto the floor
of a room. The sun is setting soon
and the sky could belong

inside a marble. Your hands
are made of leaves,
of leaving. They give

shape to light in mine. The air
is thick with cream, with anything
to say. I am kneeling

at the edge of this memory.
We walk out into the night and I dare
you to pull a fistful

of my hair and when you do
you become a child
stuffing his hands with grass.

We look up at the dark
glazed sky and thank
each individual star for coming

and I say something like a wish
into your shoulder. I go
to bed thinking *Earth plays*

hard to get when the moon
is a toenail clipping in the sky,
which means nothing,

not even if you want it to.

BEATING & ROTTING ALL AT ONCE

I'm learning a lot lately
about the visitation rights of a memory,

and how it feels to have joint custody of yourself
with yourself.

IF YOU LOVE ATTENTION MAKE SOME NOISE

I am easy to love, I am easy to love,I am easy to love, I am easy to love, I am easy to love, I am easy to love, I am easy to love, I am easy to love, I am easy to love, I am easy to love, I am easy to love, I am easy to love, I am easy to love, I am easy

DID WE WANT TOO MUCH

The year everyone was so
excited to announce.

For sale: Baby shoes.
Did not spark joy.

A kind thing I tell myself
is today was good practice

for tomorrow. Is this
not okay,

or am I not okay?
I look around at the feelings

that make up my life,
at bodies that will warm

whatever they touch.
Everything's a picture.

I love it until I don't,
go home with whoever

says my name right.
Life becomes a series

I feel obligated to finish,
and I loved it.

I loved everything.

BETWEEN US ONLY SOUND

A friend tells me that purple isn't a real color.
It's just our brains unable to decide if what

we're seeing is red or blue. I'd like to be purple,
the composite of other things that your brain

tricks your eyes into seeing. I would build dreams
with other hands. I'd be the average of every

conversation. If I reached a thought, I'd know I went
too far. But aren't all names ghosts? Is there more

between us than sound? I'll only ever get a rumor
for an answer. You can just tell.

NUDES

Nude #1. That one alone
in her living room. Finding another
way to settle an argument. Oil

diffuser on-again, off-again.
Nude #2. That one in the passenger seat,
looking like the last thing you need.

She better be finished. *In the end,*
the driver says, *it won't be cinematic.*
His won't be the last face you see.

Nude #3. That one with the touch
completely like music. They can't get inside
that feeling enough. She moves

in her own light.
Kisses into them the question
Is this how you lose her?

Nude #4. *Look who's trying*
to prove a point! a man yells at that one
specifically. She knew where to look.

Sings his name now like a ritual.
Nude #5. That one is a feral
little ruin. Heels off

and running. Quick as thought.
Nude #6. All those ones in the group chat
catching their breath.

I never liked him, one says.
That ancient proverb.
Nude #7. That one thought she was out.

Take everything, she says,
expanding as she speaks. Hit or be hit.
The locks inside her change.

Nude #9. That one winks into the void.
Sings *Tell me I'm a problem.*
Was born into this world skeptical

and hurt, and look where that got her.
Nude #10. That one got it all wrong.
Got bangs. Got steps in.

Nude #11. That one knows
too much. Watches porn she's already seen.
She'll be sorry. Leaves

without closing the door.
Nude #12. For that one, forgiveness is an option
the way luck is an option.

Every regret inside her like another life.
Pain opens like a mouth. All mercy
and teeth.

Nude #13. That one's new way of killing
needed a new way of speaking.
Like filling silence.

It would be too easy.

I SAID OKAY

what doesn't kill you
makes you mad for the rest of your life

now that I've got your attention

whatever's the rascal version of sucking meat off the bone
is what I do to the ends of all of my relationships

I am......
......that ex

whenever one of them alludes to my resting bitch personality
I buy a beauty product off my wish list

that is why my hair is so glossy and my skin is so clear

all the dumb voices we used with each other

poetry is like *not touching you!*

so much time spent thinking about
what men get away with

careful who you call crazy

you animal

no
you *machine*

new rule:
the friend who doesn't cry at lunch
picks up the check

because my god

and why not

I'm already tired tomorrow

I am laying down in spirit

I once loved a man who'd read the words
as they left his mouth

our love...
a party he left before midnight

where's the magic in that

lip plumper first thing in the morning

just to feel

I've built a career
writing poems about exes

now all my feelings look like questions

and I don't go to parties

belong to love

belong to love anyway

I am alive in the same universe
as every shade of purple

I am proud of plants

the nerve of red

I want
what I want

but what was that again

all this beauty can be exhausting

I shimmy my way into every room

why is it a crime to still feel this way

I'm nobody's crazy

I just want my hurt to come with me

okay

I said okay

I will Okay

WEEK OF WAKING THOUGHTS NO. 2

could you hold my breath for me for just a second

when you're out in the club don't think I am

[visual of ravioli food truck]

[visual of mouse cursor dragging my body to Trash]

mark yourself safe

God's transaction history for thoughts and prayers

is this just how I feel now

A WORD FOR IT

if I am speaking to you
and I suddenly stop

it is because I am considering
that everything I say lately feels like a draft

there are fresh coats of paint
and a world in my mouth!

adhesive doubts
live in the hairs on my tongue!

behind my teeth
is where I leave my dreams!

I am speaking this
like the little boy I babysit

who points to the space underneath his knees
and says *I usually like to cry in here*

I am trying to tell you
that I don't know if I come across

whether or not you hear something
if you don't have a word for it

I am a gesture
I belong mostly to movement

PEOPLE YOU MAY KNOW

everywhere people
are looking at each other

through the wrong end
of binoculars

it is so gaudy
and gruesome

getting used
to someone again

there is the first moment
when you realize

that someday you will know this person
very intimately

but it will feel like
returning to something

like you're becoming
less specific

SHOW ME

when I think of how it feels
to be in close physical proximity to you

I think of the instant gratification
of fully reducing fractions

why would they let us use each other as boundaries
to say *this is me* and *no, that's you*

I'm more of an approximation than anything else
approximately a woman

approximately an adult
approximately what I'm saying

is show me your simplest soul
(my love!)

the next time someone asks you
how old are you

I want you to ask back
how old aren't you

dissolve with me through and into
everyone else

we wait shaking at the other end
of the light

BASES

I make you read The Glass Essay

I make you follow @SheRatesDogs

you use words to describe my memories
that I use to describe my memories

you pick a cat hair off my collar

I ask you how work was

we fight

we fight

we work it out or forget we're fighting

I buy travel sizes for your place

you greet my houseplants one by one

desire replaces wonder
replaces fear
and back again

we agree *solar flare*
describes the feeling of your body
as it leaves my body

we agree *longing*
describes the feeling of our bodies
looking for one another

you say the trick is to remember
that worlds orbit heat
and you're right

you ask if you can make your heat
less your own
and then you do

RASCAL HEART

I'm coming around to you at the same time I'm coming
around to the euphemism *making love.* You hold my whole me

and I tell you the story of why I don't do acid anymore
which goes like this: Last time it took me years to relearn

how to walk outside without the overwhelming anxiety
that I might step on a bug. Also

I wanted to set my cat free outside.
Baby I love you

and I love loving you! It's okay, they can't hear us in here.
You party in the glitter-lit lighting

of my hell-yeah rascal heart. You call my name and it sounds
like something is opening up. You touch me and it is the end

of loneliness. I think you're hot!
Where I come from women are called girls no matter

how old they get. What're ya gonna do......
......I *am* a child......a child

under the covers of your love! Can't we be recklessly cute
and kiss each other's hands and agree

that the best sex we've ever had
is with each other? We have each other

and unlimited data. You song I wait in the car
to finish. You absolute place. You

oh-my-god unknowable thing. Tell me
when to stop: You make me want

to put my phone down.
You make me want to make myself a hotspot.

You make me want to try you on at home
which is redundant

because you are where I come home to now.
I don't know what it is about acid

that makes me aware that we're the only animal
that locks other animals inside rooms

but I do know that I don't need to understand something
to know what it means. You know that feeling

when you're skinny dipping and you're afraid
someone might steal your clothes? I'm sorry

I know I said I wouldn't look.

YOU UP?

You up? You think food would taste different
    if you ate it underwater? How long you think
        magic hour lasts for on Neptune? What do
            you think cellulite would look like on fish?
                Can you believe olives are a fruit? You ever
            notice that *OM* is—okay, yes, the sound of the
        universe, but also the sound literally every
    little kid makes when speaking into a fan?
You up? You ever think about how English
    maybe isn't our first language? The way
        I'm sitting right now is my first language.
            The way I bring my hand to your jawline is my
        first language. The way I become movement
    inside your hands is my first language.
You up? Did your mom ever make you talk
    to shit? My mom imbued life into every
        corner and crumb of my small world, and
            now as an adult woman my heart breaks
                every time I find an empty snail shell,
        or for the worms on rainy mornings who
    aren't going to have enough time to make
    it to the other side of the driveway.
You up? You ever feel like when you fall in
    love it's just this feeling of having known
        someone before, but also of wanting to find
            out how much time you can kill counting the
                pockets and handles you can make together
            with your bodies? There's the age-old that
    goes *Love is forgetting about death*, but when

I'm with you I also forget about the internet.
You up? How do you arrange your apps, by the way?
    What's your favorite shade of blue? Sometimes
        when men talk about themselves I like to imagine
            I'm transcribing their monologues in my head, and
                I like to picture how many page breaks I have to
                    make. I file them into a mental folder called *Brief*
                    Interviews with Hideous Men. But with you, I would
                take the things you say and I would stick them
            inside a leaf book. Did I ever tell you about the
    time a dude asked me to be his scribe for him?
You up? Why are people who love each
    other still sending each other heart emojis
        when there's the shooting star emoji? the
            sunset-on-the-horizon emoji? I want to
                trace an excel sheet over your body and
            share it with you on Google Drive. I want
    to do with you what night does to the
smell of the ground by morning.

MAKE ME

a body has no angle
    no plot

but the way you move your hands makes me
    so aware that we come

from one long lineage of friction
    and skin

millions of moments of having
    so much love

our bodies didn't know where else
    to put it all down

but touch is a balding gesture
    watch this

BEING ON THE PHONE WITH YOU

you called to tell me that when
we are both online it is like a
staring contest

that you associate my voice
with the sound of WhatsApp
notifications more than with my
own voice now

that your mom can't shut up
about World War II

she watched a documentary
last weekend and works it into
every conversation

being on the phone with you is
better than REM sleep

better than a full eight hours

better than the watery nightcap
stationed at the edge of my
nightstand

and better than any dream you
could've interrupted

like the one when you wouldn't
let me sleep in your bed with
you until I let you pierce my
nose on both sides

or the one when I was walking
around with nothing but a bag
of spinach in my backpack and
I stopped to ask Malia Obama
to help you with your
nosebleed

and to tell you the truth

I consider it an investment for
the hours I spend in the
mornings and afternoons
waiting for you to wake up on
the other side of the world

which is actually the best part
of my day

I look at a message from you
and think that from August
until ??? we are as much our
phone lives as we are our
physical lives

maybe even more so

and I live in the space
maintained by software
updates

and in the quickness of
satellites

and where we can be quiet

strangely when my phone
battery dies everything seems
a little brighter

like I have been groping
through a dream and someone
has just turned the lights on

and I immediately want to jump
back into the glossy cracked
surface of my dead phone
screen

like when Blue ska-doos into a
picture frame and Steve follows
her

I want to become the
smoothness and coldness of
your phone

and hang on your thigh all day

and not because I'm the
jealous one and becoming your
phone would grant me access
to your notifications

but because I would be treated
by your hands

or because there would be
moments when you would
desperately try to turn me on

and because you would reach
for me when you didn't have
anything else to do

POP UP TRUST ISSUES

1.

when I was very small
my grandpa would take out his dentures
and chase me around his apartment with them

2.

a friend tells me
she eats one bag of frozen grapes
per day

IF YOU LOVE IT SO MUCH

for Layne and Mark

If you love it so much   why don't you be open with it
about your personal boundaries
and respect its boundaries
in return?

If you love it so much   why don't you give it a healthy amount
of space to pursue its own interests
and come back to it refreshed
and ready to share your experiences?

If you love it so much   why don't you create some new
memories together?

If you love it so much   why don't you develop a realistic view
of long-term monogamy
and communicate your expectations
but also your hopes with it?

If you love it so much   why don't you be careful with your words
when quarreling with it?

If you love it so much   why don't you address problems
and misunderstandings
with it immediately?

If you love it so much   why don't you give it honest,
specific compliments?

If you love it so much	why don't you be fair and generous
in moments of conflict?

If you love it so much	why don't you mindfully recommit to it
every day?

If you love it so much	why don't you make an effort
to play together once in a while
instead of emphasizing
perpetual productivity?

If you love it so much	why don't you set aside one evening
per week for a date night to keep
the romance fresh?

If you love it so much	why don't you use *we language*
and not *me language*
when discussing future plans
and aspirations?

If you love it so much	why don't you let it bend the corners
of your pages until your mouth
is made of stars?

why don't you unfold into it
like you're bringing it the news?

why don't you wait for it
the way a throat waits,
ready with syllables?

why don't you take off your shadow
for it to wear like silk?

FIGHT (I KNOW YOU CAN HEAR ME)

The one that's made of time.
We took turns naming things,

which is the traditional way
lovers sharpen one another.

Point: Remember when I drove your car
for you so you could dry your nails

out the window?
What do you call that?

Counterpoint: Somewhere in the world
a snake gets lost in an endless

tunnel of its own skin after shedding
doesn't quite go according to plan.

Nobody knows how to feel
about it. What is prey?

Well, what is plunder?
A stillness goes viral as the room fractures

into danger between us.
Come on, it's late, you say finally,

and with such sudden gentleness
I mistake you for dawn.

WHAT KIND OF LOVE IS THAT
(I KNOW WHAT I'M DOING)

today the news
teaches me new ways
to feel

and I thought
   I should have
   thought
to ask you
   is what I think

that night I dreamt
and in the dream I left
   was leaving
a room
for the last time

but I will make you soft
   again

I have made myself soft
   new again
for you

today the news
and the world I ignore it
    or I try to

    maybe

I did what
    of course
I had to

we went to similar things
and now in the night
we meet like this

but we've got
to stop
    (my love)

today the news
but I don't listen

   so tired

what kind of love
is a free country?

or if I kept feeding you
you could make more
of yourself
   could you?

what kind of love
is that?

that with time
he finds me again
   and in
   someone else!

but I
   oh I
am full
of joy

today the news
doesn't scare me
    does it?
anymore
    nothing will

whatever animal
I thought I fed
into the night
is over now
    over there

I have seen the price
of hunger and look
what he's done
    what he *did*
to me

but your hurt
I thought I knew it
from somewhere
    it looked
    so much
    like mine

whatever song is at
the back of your throat
I hope it one day
sings to me
    oh sing
    to me

today the news

    are you feeling it
    yet? do you feel
    anything?

I am still with you
in that part of the night
but you
    you
are not

what is taking so long?
    what is it you want
    to say to me?

in the back of the morning
I called out your name
but you said
    only said
what was that for?

so I think
could you love me?
have you thought
you could learn to?

oh call out my name
and I will raise this song
to you:

only war is war
(my love) and I
    I
know
what I'm doing

today the news
wants to know what
we first called ourselves

and I think
    keep thinking
you are only all I feel!
    yes! it's you
    whom I feel!

your beauty has nothing
to do with me
I don't wish for it to
    why would you
    even ask that?

and though I've loved
I haven't been her
since two nudes ago

I had hoped
there would be more
    now I just hope
    it will be different
    soon

today the news
stays
    won't you?

I have been possible
    once
    and for all

I who can't fight
    feel it
    even name it
anymore

that's how it has to feel

or I have thought so
I have thought
    that
out of the light
comes what I think

and what I think
is I
    would
love you

EMOTION STANDS FOR ELECTRONIC MOTION

I thought

that you'd

come back

to me

I thought

that you'd

you'd

come back

to me

REBOUND (ONE MORE TIME)

does it make me endless

if I've been shivered
into blur or stencil

by his and his hands

morning dropped
and it was wonderful

he'd touched me like he had
no other possessions in the world

took turns rocking along
to the credits of the sky
rolling above us

all with the night left open

and anyone's guess from there

you know lately
whenever I go looking for something
to return me to private hunger

I enjoy getting reduced to parts

how else would you be able to see yourself
from as many points of view as possible
at the same time?

they go on anyway

shaking their mouths at me

cut from cut

light from light

instead what I found
on the other side of the night

was that cold is a feeling
you have to pay attention to

that when they ask you
to cast your sadness out

like a net
to catch more shadow

it's all so you know what it's like
to feel useful

I mean really

can you imagine

o! glory

o...everyone

teach me which
of these bad feelings
are my own

how to stop playing with words
that are more theirs than mine

that when time opens
again and again

to stay where the sound is

still I go so far as to think

you were what blessed me back
to the quiet in myself

how it brings me to song

to storm

even now

NOTES

YOU ANIMAL: The lines "my loneliness / was killing me / *aaaand I*" and "I still believe" are taken from the song "Hit Me Baby (One More Time)" by Britney Spears.

HARD FEELINGS + LOVELESS: These titles are taken from the song "Hard Feelings / Loveless" by Lorde.

CALL IT WHAT YOU WANT: The line "you want for quiet to be a matter of rolling up all the sidewalks outside" was taken from a line in the children's novel *Why Is This Night Different from All Other Nights? (All the Wrong Questions Book 4)* by Lemony Snicket.

NUDES: This poem was written after a portion of the poem "The Glass Essay" by Anne Carson. The lines "Kisses into them the question / *Is this how you lose her?*" is a reference to the book *This Is How You Lose Her* by Junot Diaz. The lyric "*Tell me I'm a problem*" is from the song "No Angel" by Beyoncé. An image in this poem is taken from "Amour Fou" (*The Sopranos*, 2001).

I SAID OKAY: The final line "okay / I said okay / I will Okay" is a reference to "yes I said yes I will Yes"—the final line of the novel *Ulysses* by James Joyce.

WEEK OF WAKING THOUGHTS NO. 2: The line "when you're out in the club don't think I am" is a reference to the song "Don't Think I'm Not" by Kandi.

RASCAL HEART: This poem was written after "Planet of the Apes" by Hera Lindsay Bird. The phrase "hell-yeah rascal heart" was adapted from "collective HELLYEAH heart" in Layne Ransom's poem "Wolves."

YOU UP?: The line "I file them into a mental folder called *Brief Interviews with Hideous Men*" is a reference to the collection of short stories *Brief Interviews with Hideous Men* by David Foster Wallace.

FIGHT (I KNOW YOU CAN HEAR ME): The point/counterpoint structure of this poem was taken from "Four Fights" by Natalie Shapero.

WHAT KIND OF LOVE IS THAT (I KNOW WHAT I'M DOING): An earlier version of this poem was written after "At Night the States" by Alice Notley.

REBOUND (ONE MORE TIME): The title of this poem is a reference to the song "Hit Me Baby (One More Time)" by Britney Spears. The lines "cut from cut" and "light from light" are references to the prayer "The Nicene Creed."

ACKNOWLEDGMENTS

Thank you to the editors of the following journals and presses where earlier versions of many of these poems first appeared: *Alien Mouth, Cosmonauts Avenue,* Metatron Press, Monster House Press, *Potluck Mag, Shabby Doll House, Spy Kids Review, Sundress Publications, Voicemail Poems,* and *The Wanderer.* Special thanks to Ashley Obscura, Bükem Reitmayer, and Lucy K Shaw for their friendship and early belief in my work.

Thank you to my favorite poets Hera Lindsay Bird, Kimmy Walters, and Jakob Maier for their thoughtful and generous advance praise of *That Ex.*

Shooting star and sunset-on-the-horizon emojis to the friends and readers who offered encouragement and feedback on earlier versions of this book: Aidan Ryan, Ashley Obscura, Caroline Rayner, Jakob Maier, Janet McNally, Julianne Neely, Lucy K Shaw, Matthew Bookin, Monika Woods, Noah Falck, and Spencer Madsen.

Thank you to my *Peach Mag* team for their rascal hearts: Aeon Ginsberg, Bre Kiblin, C. C. Camuglia, D. Arthur, Jakob Maier, Julia Beck, Kelly Xio, Liz Bowen, Matthew Bookin, Mickey Harmon, Rax King, RE Katz, Sage Enderton, Sebastian Castillo, Sennah Yee, and Shayna Kiblin.

Thank you to the readers, writers, curators, booksellers, arts administrators, and patrons of Buffalo's LIT CITY community for making this the best damn place to write a book. Special thanks to the folks at Talking Leaves...Books and Just Buffalo Literary Center for their leadership and support.

Thank you to my family for their faith and pride: Camille Toarmino, Patricia Murphy, and Russ Toarmino.

Thank you to Bug, whose love is still the biggest and best feeling I've ever known.

Thank u to the exes I've loved, lost, and let go. Next.

Thank you, Mark Cugini. For making this and so much else possible in our one world.

This book is dedicated to my friends.